Table of Contents

Legendary Locations 4
King Tutankhamun's Tomb, Egypt 6
Halema'uma'u Crater, Hawaii 12
Lake Guatavita, Colombia 18
Sherwood Forest, England 24
Memory Game 30
Index 31
After-Reading Questions 31
Activity 31
About the Author 32

Legendary Locations

Halemaʻumaʻu Crater, Hawaii

Lake Guatavita, Colombia

ARCTIC OCEAN
NORTH AMERICA
ATLANTIC OCEAN
PACIFIC OCEAN
AFRICA
SOUTH AMERICA
ATLANTIC OCEAN
SOUTHERN OCEAN

Have you ever heard of a lost city of gold? Or the curse of a pharaoh? Some of the most fascinating stories have roots in real places all over the world. Find out where these places are and the stories that surround them!

King Tutankhamun's Tomb, Egypt

King Tutankhamun is popularly known as King Tut. He became the king, or pharoah, of Egypt around 1314 B.C.E. He was only nine years old. His father had not been well-liked. He changed the religion of the kingdom and moved the capital to a new place. This upset the people of Egypt, who liked the way things were.

King Tutankhamun's Tomb, Egypt

King Tut died at age nineteen. The pharaohs who came after him acted like he didn't exist. This is probably because of how much King Tut's father was disliked.

The Death of the King

No one is sure what exactly killed King Tut. It is said that he had poor health his entire life. When scientists inspected his body, they found a broken leg and multiple infections. All of this probably contributed to his death.

Because there were no records of him, King Tut's tomb was forgotten. When it was rediscovered in 1922, it was the most intact tomb ever found. There were rooms filled with treasures. Murals, perfumes, toys, jewelry, and more were all found untouched.

King Tutankhamun's Tomb, Egypt

Rumors of the curse of King Tut started quickly after the discovery of his tomb. One of the men at the tomb's opening ceremony, George Herbert, died two months later. A few more people who were there when the tomb was opened also died unexpectedly. Newspapers went wild with stories of the "pharaoh's curse." The deaths were likely **coincidences**, but people loved the story of the curse.

🚩 **coincidences** (koh-IN-si-duhns-iz): surprising or remarkable events that seem to happen by chance

Halema'uma'u Crater, Hawaii

The Hawaiian goddess of volcanoes is Pele, or Pelehonuamea. Hawaiian legends say that Pele came to Hawaii by crossing the ocean in a boat. She shaped the land of Hawaii with her digging stick. Where her stick dug in, it created volcanic **craters**. Eventually, Pele made her home in the crater of Halema'uma'u at the top of the Kīlauea Volcano.

🚩 **craters** (KRAY-turz): the mouths of volcanoes

Halemaʻumaʻu Crater, Hawaii

Pele is described as having a temper. When volcanoes erupt, it is Pele showing her anger. Many who believe in the power of Pele also see beauty in the eruptions. They look at it as Pele creating and destroying. Pele is often called *Tutu* Pele, meaning grandmother.

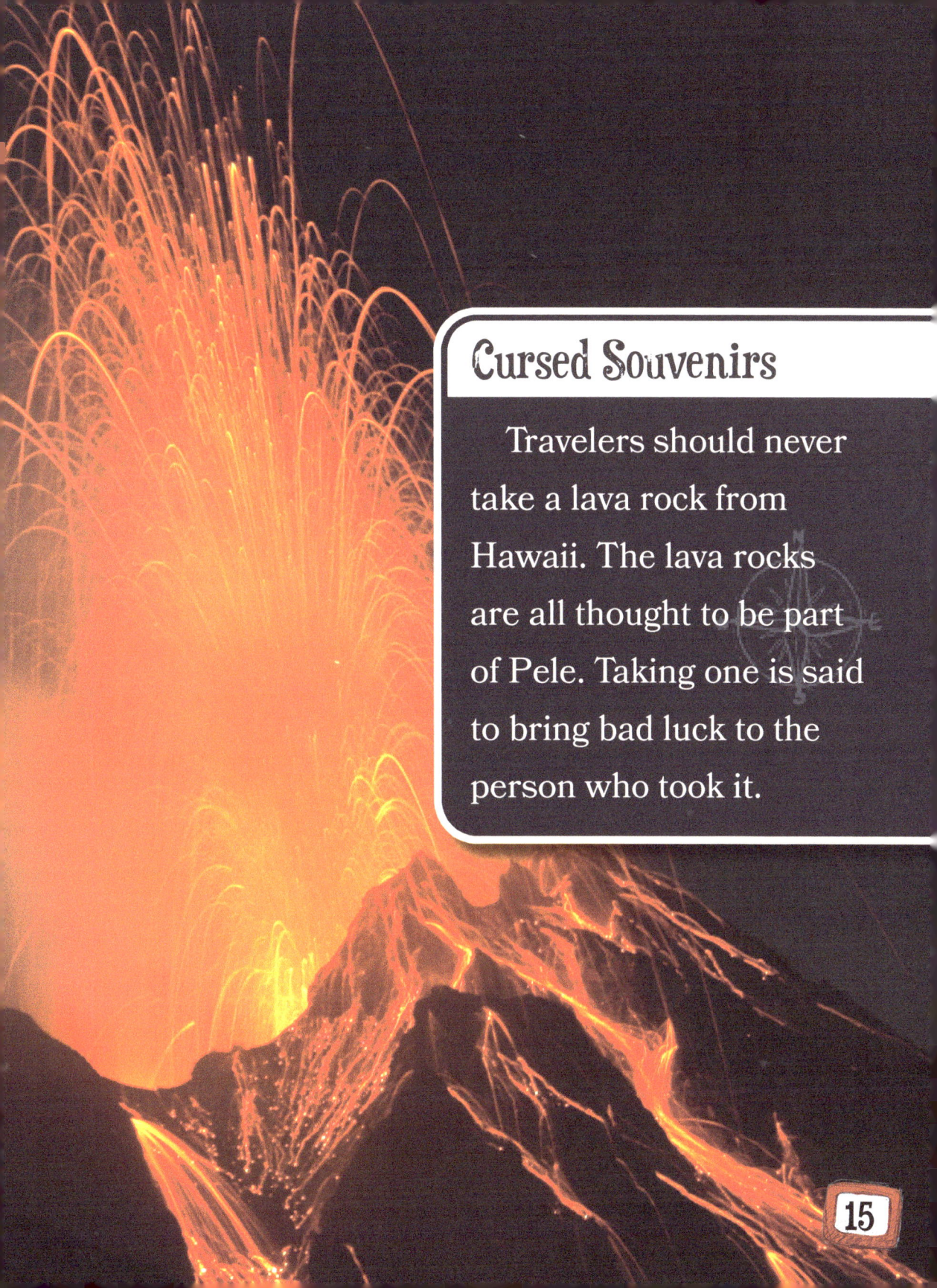

Cursed Souvenirs

Travelers should never take a lava rock from Hawaii. The lava rocks are all thought to be part of Pele. Taking one is said to bring bad luck to the person who took it.

Halemaʻumaʻu Crater, Hawaii

People bring gifts, called *hoʻokupu*, to Pele that they set near the Halemaʻumaʻu crater. Traditional *hoʻokupu* include pork, bananas, flowers from the *ʻōhiʻa-lehua* tree, and red berries from the *ʻōhelo ʻai* plant.

Lake Guatavita, Colombia

The myth of El Dorado was started by European explorers. At first, it was a story about a very rich man. But over time, El Dorado came to mean a lost city of gold.

This myth made the Spanish want to explore and **colonize** the Americas even more than they already did. This colonizing hurt the people already thriving there.

colonize (KAH-luh-nize): to establish a new colony in a place

Lake Guatavita, Colombia

The Muisca people are an important part of the beginning of El Dorado. The Muisca were living in South America before the Spanish invaded. The Muisca had a population of more than 500,000 people.

Statues of Muisca kings can be found in Colombia today.

They had a powerful economy, their own political systems, culture, sports, and religion. Over time, the Spanish took over. They stole land, abused people, and forced the Muisca people to **assimilate**.

🚩 **assimilate** (uh-SIM-uhl-ate): to absorb into the cultural tradition of a group

Lake Guatavita, Colombia

Some Spanish explorers saw a Muisca ceremony that took place when a new leader was chosen. This ceremony is what started the legend of El Dorado.

Gold artifacts from the Muisca people can be seen in a museum.

The new Muisca chief, surrounded by priests, would take a raft out onto Lake Guatavita. Everyone on the raft would be covered in gold. When they got to the middle of the lake, the new leader would throw gold objects into the lake as an **offering** to the gods.

Draining the Lake

In 1545, the Spanish tried to drain Lake Guatavita. They found hundreds of gold objects on the lake's edge. But they weren't able to drain it enough to search the middle of the lake where the best of the treasure was supposed to be.

offering (AW-fur-ing): a gift given as an act of worship

Sherwood Forest, England

The legend of Robin Hood has been around since the 19th century. Robin Hood was said to be an outlaw who stole from the rich to give to the poor. Historians have not been able to find the original Robin Hood. The tale seemed to have spread through **oral tradition** in poetry, stories, and songs.

An Outlaw Name

Historians have found old criminal records for many different men named Robin Hood. It is believed to have been used as a common fake name for outlaws.

oral tradition (OR-uhl truh-DISH-uhn): a community's stories and beliefs passed down by word of mouth

Sherwood Forest, England

Over time Sherwood Forest became tied to Robin Hood. The laws were strict around the forest. Common people were not allowed to hunt or chop down trees.

This upset the locals. They were not allowed to use the resources the forest provided. This also made the forest wild – the perfect setting for Robin Hood to hide.

Sherwood Forest, England

28

The Major Oak is a popular attraction in the Sherwood Forest. This tree is said to be anywhere from 800 to 1,100 years old. The Major Oak often acts as the home of Robin Hood and his men in the stories. They were said to sleep under the branches and hide inside the trunk.

Memory Game

Look at the pictures. What do you remember reading on the pages where each image appeared?

Index

culture 21
El Dorado 18, 20, 22
King Tut 6, 8, 9, 11
outlaw(s) 25
Pele 13, 14, 15, 16
Robin Hood 25, 26, 27, 29,
tomb 6, 8, 9, 10, 11
volcano(es) 13, 14

After-Reading Questions

1. Why didn't people like King Tut's father?
2. What are three things that were found in King Tut's tomb?
3. What are two traditional gifts, or hoʻokupu, people offer to Pele?
4. What Muisca ceremony started the myth of El Dorado?
5. How did the stories of Robin Hood spread?

Activity

What types of legends are there in the place where you live? Research legends in your city or country. Choose one and write a description of the legend and place.

About the Author

Hailey Scragg loves visiting and learning about new places and stories. She hopes to one day see some of these legendary locations. Until then she will keep exploring her city of Columbus, Ohio with her husband and dog.

© 2021 Rourke Educational Media

All rights reserved. No part of this book may be reproduced or utilized in any form or by any means, electronic or mechanical including photocopying, recording, or by any information storage and retrieval system without permission in writing from the publisher.

www.rourkeeducationalmedia.com

PHOTO CREDITS: Cover, page 1, 30: ©Manu1174; pages 6-7: ©Merydolla; pages 8-9, 30: ©Jaroslav Moravcik; pages 10-11: ©Nick Brundle; page 12-13, 30: © ferrantraite; page 13: ©Marlon Trottmann / Alamy Stock Photo; page 14-15:©AZ68; page 16: ©Milaski; page 16-17, 30: ©Milaski; page 18-19: ©ESB Professional; page 20: ©Mark Pitt Images; page 21: ©Mark Pitt Images; page 22: ©Mark Green; page 22-23, 30: ©Simon Pittet; page 24-25: ©BrettCharlton; page 26-27: ©Ian Bracegirdle; page 27: ©Tutti Frutti; page 28-29, 30: ©travellinglight

Edited by: Madison Capitano
Cover design by: J.J. Giddings
Interior design by: J.J. Giddings

Library of Congress PCN Data

Places of Legend / Hailey Scragg
 (Hidden, Lost, and Discovered)
  ISBN 978-1-73164-333-9 (hard cover)
  ISBN 978-1-73164-297-4 (soft cover)
  ISBN 978-1-73164-365-0 (e-Book)
  ISBN 978-1-73164-397-1 (e-Pub)
Library of Congress Control Number: 2020945278

Rourke Educational Media
Printed in the United States of America
02-0942211957O

CPSIA information can be obtained
at www.ICGtesting.com
Printed in the USA
BVHW020602030422
R133538000lB/R133538PG633120BVX00002B/1